It is 2012. The world's leaders gather in Brazil for a meeting, the Rio+20 Summit. They have come to discuss the future of the world, which is facing an ever worsening environmental crisis.

One after another, they give speeches, but no one says anything new.

As evening falls, it is the President of Uruguay's turn to speak. José Mujica steps up to the podium, wearing a simple shirt with no tie. He is known as "the world's poorest president."

He has this name because as president, José Mujica donates almost all of his salary to the poor.

When he was elected, he decided that he would not live in the presidential palace. Instead, he would continue to live with his wife on their farm, growing flowers and vegetables. And he would drive his trusty old car, instead of being driven in the official, presidential one.

What counts for President Mujica is what needs to be done, not the appearance of things. His countrymen love him and call him Pepe, which means Grandpa.

As Mujica starts to speak, no one seems especially interested in hearing from the leader of such a small country. But by the time he has finished, the room will be filled with thunderous applause.

THE WORLD'S POOREST PRESIDENT
SPEAKS OUT

Based on Uruguay President José Mujica's
2012 Speech to the United Nations Conference
on Sustainable Development

Editor
YOSHIMI KUSABA

Illustrator
GAKU NAKAGAWA

Translator
ANDREW WONG

Enchanted Lion Books
NEW YORK

Leaders of the world, thank you for gathering here today.
My thanks as well to the Brazilian people and to Madame President
for hosting us here in Rio, and to those of you who have already
spoken, thank you for your commitment and good faith.

Now, let us ask: What is the future for humanity? What path should
we take? As leaders we have come together, united in spirit,
to talk about our future. We all know that things cannot go on
as they are. Something must change!

I am going to speak forcefully this evening and ask some hard questions.

This entire afternoon, we have talked about how to live in harmony with nature, how to rid the world of poverty.

But what has really been going on inside our heads all this time? Haven't our thoughts still been about how to make more money? And how to create a world where we can have access to whatever we want?

Let me ask you this: What would happen to this planet if everyone in India owned the same number of cars as every family in Germany? Would there be enough air left for us to breathe?

To state it more clearly: Does the world have enough resources for the entire human race, seven to eight billion of us, to live like the Western societies that keep making and buying more than they need?

Is it possible? Or are we going to have to face some very different problems one day?

We humans created civilization, and its progress has been simply amazing. Life is now so convenient for so many. It's never been as easy to get more and better things.

We have created a civilization based on a system where we sell things to make money, which we use to buy whatever we want, and then we buy some more.

And since we can now buy and sell our goods across the world's markets, we find places where people will make things cheaply, and we sell them for far more elsewhere.

But we must ask ourselves: Are we using our system well? Or are we being run by it?

We compete ruthlessly, each to become richer than the next. Can we really talk about the solidarity of humankind and kindness to each other, or even togetherness, when we are constantly competing to outdo each other?

This meeting should not be a waste of time. Rather, the opposite, because we face enormous challenges ahead. But first, we must realize that the real problem is not climate change.

Humanity is in grave danger because of the system we have created. The problem is in how we have come to live our lives.

How do we live our lives?
Let's take it simply.
Why were we born?

Was it to pursue economic growth
and progress?
No.

We came into the world to live in such a
way as to find happiness on this planet.

Life is over in the blink of an eye.
Nothing is more valuable.

But what happens when we spend our lives working
to buy more than we need, and end up finding that
life has passed us by too quickly?

Today's society is driven by production and consumption. This cycle must continue to keep the gears of our economies moving. If they stop turning, the money will stop flowing. And when that happens, the dreaded recession will strike us all.

But that is not the real monster. The real monster is called desire. Desire consumes our world.

To satisfy this monstrous desire, we must make things that do not last—because we must keep selling.

A regular light bulb burns out after about 1,000 hours.
Some can last 10,000 or even 20,000 hours.

But we do not make such things. Why?

Because our system requires us to keep buying and selling.
We work to buy things, and then we throw them away
after a while. Such is the culture of our civilization.

We are part of this vicious cycle, which is why I say
humanity is in grave danger. This is why we must find
a way to build a different culture.

I am not saying that we should go back into our caves.
Nor am I asking anyone to turn back the clock.

Rather, I am saying that we cannot continue to live as we do
today. It is time for us to rethink what we seek in life.

As the old thinkers Epicurus and Seneca defined it, and
as the Aymara people, indigenous to South America, do:
It is not the one who has little who is poor. The one who is
truly poor is the one who needs infinitely more, the one
who is never satisfied.

This common wisdom holds the key for humanity today.

As the leader of my small nation of Uruguay, I respect our agreements, and I know some things I have said are hard to swallow.

But we must realize that humanity is in danger not just because of the lack of drinking water or our aggression toward nature. The danger is rooted in what we have come to seek to make us happy.

We must change our way of life.

I am from a small country that is blessed with sufficient natural resources. We rear 13 million excellent cows and about 10 million superb sheep. Nearly all of our rich land can be farmed. We export crops, dairy products, and meat.

In the past, my countrymen worked long hours. But we fought hard to shorten the working day to eight hours. Today, Uruguayans need to work only six hours a day.

But some people work those six hours and take up a second job, so they end up working even more than before.

Why? Because they have to pay off debts—for motorcycles, cars, and other things they borrowed money to buy. By the time they realize what has happened, they are like me, old and rheumatic, and their journey through life is coming to an end.

And then that person might ask, "Is this where life has taken me?"

My message is very simple: Economic growth and progress must add to human happiness, not take away from it.

These are the building blocks of our happiness as humans: having satisfying relationships with others; raising children; making friends; spreading love in the world.

We must make economic growth and progress help us experience these because . . .

Shared human happiness is the greatest treasure of all.

If we appreciate the beauty of nature and life itself and care for our world, we will be able to continue to live well as humans on this planet.

Thank you.

José MUJICA

A staunch Leftist and former guerilla, José Alberto "Pepe" Mujica Cordano served as the 40th president of Uruguay between 2010–2015. While he was in office, he donated nearly 90% of his salary to charities working in support of small business owners and the poor. He delivered the speech featured in this book to the United Nations Conference on Sustainable Development in Rio de Janeiro in 2012. He later became something of a folk hero in Japan, where this book was first published.

Illustrator | Gaku NAKAGAWA

An ordained monk, Gaku Nakagawa became an illustrator in 1996. He has been featured in the international magazine *Monocle* and in a special feature on World Illustrators published by Taschen. He has received numerous awards and recognitions.

Translator | Andrew WONG

Born in Singapore, Andrew Wong now lives in Tokyo, having spent six years away from major cities, living in Stirling, Scotland, and later Fukui, Japan. It was his experiences there that helped to hone his thinking about different ways of life. His passion to share stories has led to his work as a translator.

Editor (original Japanese edition) | Yoshimi KUSABA

Editors (English-language edition) | Claudia Zoe BEDRICK and Kate FINNEY

www.enchantedlion.com

First English language edition published in 2020 by Enchanted Lion Books
67 West St, Suite 403, Brooklyn, NY 11222

English-language translation copyright © 2020 by Enchanted Lion Books

English-language edition copyright © 2020 by Enchanted Lion Books

Japanese-language edition copyright ©2014 by Yoshimi Kusaba, Gaku Nakagawa

First published in Japan in 2014 as *Sekai De Ichiban Mazushī Daitōryō No Supīchi*
by Choubunsha Publishing Co., Ltd. Tokyo.

English translation rights arranged with KADOKAWA CORPORATION, Tokyo
through JAPAN UNI AGENCY, INC., Tokyo.

Book design by Eugenia Mello.

All rights reserved under International and Pan-American Copyright Conventions

A CIP record is on file with the Library of Congress

ISBN: 978-1-59270-289-3

Printed in 2020 by R.R. Donnelley Asia Print Solutions